A Walk Through Edinburgh's New Town

Eric Melvin

ISBN- 10: 1500122017

ISBN-13: 978-1-9196513-1-6

DEDICATION & THANKS

I would like to express my sincere thanks to Alison Stoddart of the City of Edinburgh Council City Libraries Department for her help in identifying photographs from the excellent Capital Collections.

Thanks are also due to Ryan Clee of the National Galleries of Scotland for providing images from the National Collections.

I am also grateful to Peter Stubbs of Edinburgh Photos and Ian Smith of Scottish Pictures for allowing me to include images from Thomas Shepherd's *'Modern Athens Displayed.'* In addition I have included photos from Peter's site of the Mound and the Dome.

I am very much indebted to my brother Alan Melvin who has produced the maps to guide the reader through each section of the walk. He has also brought his considerable editorial talents into play. I am very much in his debt.

Also a sincere 'thank you' to my cousin Lesley Winton for her help and expertise in taking this project forward.

Finally I would like to particularly thank my dear wife Lynda Melvin. Her skilled 'critical eye' and constant encouragement have both been invaluable.

I would like to dedicate this book to my son
Graeme Melvin.

Contents

Illustration Credits

With the kind permission of the City of Edinburgh
Council – Libraries. www.capitalcollections.org.uk
ps. 2, 3, 5, 6, 7, 58, 59, 62, 65, 71, 89

With the kind permission of the National Galleries
of Scotland
Picture.library@nationalgalleries.org
ps. 15, 20, 36, 39, 44, 45, 54, 68, 74, 77

Eric Melvin
eric.melvin@btinternet.com
ps. 1, 9, 10, 11, 12, 19, 21, 22, 25, 26, 27, 28, 32, 33, 34,
35, 38, 40, 43, 46, 47, 48, 51, 52, 53, 57, 64, 66, 67, 69,
70, 73, 76, 81, 82, 83, 84, 85, 86, 87, 90, 91, 92

Reproduced with grateful acknowledgement to Ian
Smith
ian@scottishpictures.com
ps. 17, 30 (and front cover),42, 55, 60

Reproduced with grateful acknowledgement to
Peter Stubbs
peter.stubbs@edinphotoorg.uk
ps. 13, 23, 37, 49, 50, 72, 78

1. INTRODUCTION

The New Town from Edinburgh Castle

Edinburgh's New Town is perhaps the finest surviving example of 18th century town planning to be found anywhere in the world. The New Town's status was recognised in 1995 when, along with the equally famous Old Town, it was designated as a World Heritage Site by UNESCO.

The man responsible more than any other for driving forward this dream of what even then was styled Edinburgh's New Town, was Lord Provost George Drummond. He was born in Perthshire in 1687 and came to Edinburgh to work as a Commissioner of Customs. He was first elected to the position of Lord Provost in 1725. His last appointment, his sixth, was in 1762 when he had reached the age of 75.

Lord Provost George Drummond

As Lord Provost, George Drummond worked hard to bring about improvements to Edinburgh. He persuaded his fellow-citizens to raise the money for a new Infirmary started in 1738 as well as for the Royal Exchange, (now the City Chambers) in the High Street started in 1755. His dream though was to relieve the pressure on the over-crowded historic Old Town of Edinburgh and to build a New Town.

By the middle of the 18th century, Edinburgh was bursting at the seams. Some 60000 were crammed into the historic Old Town enclosed by its ancient Flodden Wall. Many were living in old tenements - some of which were an incredible fourteen stories high. Visitors to the Old Town were definitely not impressed by the overcrowding and the filth.

An 18th century English traveller, John Taylor, recorded that:

"Every street shows the nastiness of the inhabitants; the excrement lies in heaps. The smell was so bad we were forced to hold our noses, and to take care where we stepped. We had to walk in the middle of the streets for fear of an accident on our heads."

This *"accident on our heads"* was of course a reference to the Edinburgh practice of *'Gardyloo!'* (from the French,*"Watch out for the water")* whereby household waste was simply thrown out of the windows to be cleared up during the night by scavengers. The smell must have been truly awful! No wonder then that the Town Council and leading citizens turned their thoughts to a New Town on the green, open lands across the Nor' Loch – the old defensive water barrier lying to the north beneath the walls of Edinburgh Castle.

An Old Town Close

In 1775 the Reverend Thomas Sommerville recalled a conversation with George Drummond as they looked out over the Nor' Loch to the open fields beyond:

"You Mr Somerville are a young man and may probably live, though I will not, to see all these fields covered with houses, forming a splendid and magnificent city. To the accomplishment of this nothing more is necessary than draining the Nor' Loch and providing a proper access from the Old Town. I have never lost sight of this object since the year 1725 when I was first elected Provost."

For Drummond's dream to be realised, permission had to be obtained from Parliament in London to extend Edinburgh's ancient boundaries. In 1752 a group of leading citizens published '*Proposals for carrying out certain Public Works in the City of Edinburgh*'. These included the extension of the burgh's royalty to take in the open countryside to the north of the Nor' Loch. This was not finally approved until 1767. Despite this delay, Drummond drove forward his ambitious vision for the city.

In 1763 work started on draining the waters of the Nor' Loch which covered the area now occupied by Princes Street Gardens and the Waverley Station. In 1765 Drummond laid the foundation stone for the North Bridge. This was his last public act. He died the following year. Unfortunately poor construction work resulted in part of the bridge collapsing in 1769. Five people were killed. Although work was started to repair the bridge, it was not completed until 1778. Understandably, Edinburgh citizens were at first very reluctant to risk crossing the new North Bridge.

The North Bridge 1817

This New Town was the result of a competition organised by the Town Council in 1766. The competition was won by a young, previously-unknown 23 year old architect, James Craig. His design was a simple 'grid iron' of parallel streets balanced at either end by elegant squares each with a grand church. The original plan included a canal to be built on the site of the Nor' Loch. This though was never carried out.

At the insistence of King George III, this New Town was to be a celebration of Great Britain and the royal house of Hanover. The principal street, running along a natural ridge of higher ground was to be named George Street after the King himself and his son the Prince of Wales. Hanover Street celebrated the family name of the King and Frederick Street after the King's second son the Duke of York. (The *'Grand Old Duke of York'* of Nursery-Rhyme fame.)

The original plan shown to George III had the southern street, in the shadow of the Castle and the Old Town, named 'St Giles Street' after Edinburgh's patron saint. King George though was not best pleased with this suggestion! He is reported as having stamped his feet and shouted:

"Hey! Hey! What! What! St Giles Street! Never do! Never do!"

To be fair to the King, he was not being anti - Edinburgh or anti-Scottish. St Giles was also the patron saint of lepers and beggars and the district of St Giles in London was a hotbed of crime and loose living. So the name was changed to Princes Street after the King's two eldest sons. The two squares were to be named after the patron saints of Scotland (St Andrew) and England (St George). Unfortunately there already was a George Square in Edinburgh so the western square was named instead after George's wife and his eldest daughter, both called Charlotte.

James Craig

The original plan had George Street 'balanced' at either end by two churches – St Andrew's and St George's. But, as we shall see, this was to be thwarted by the actions of a selfish banker, Sir Lawrence Dundas, who purchased the land earmarked for St Andrew's Church, planned for the east end of St Andrew Square, and built his own luxurious townhouse there.

Between the principal streets, two lanes were to be built for tradesmen and servants with stabling for the horses and the carriages of the wealthy residents. These were to be named after the emblems of Scotland and England – Thistle Street and Rose Street.

Work started on this first phase of the New Town in 1767 and was not finished until 1811 when Charlotte Square was completed.

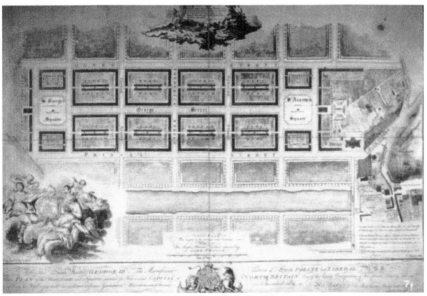

James Craig's Plan for the New Town

The North Bridge and Register House c 1779

MAP 1

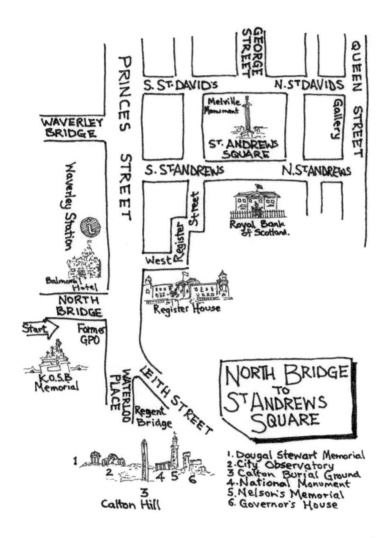

NORTH BRIDGE TO St ANDREWS SQUARE

1. Dougal Stewart Memorial
2. City Observatory
3. Calton Burial Ground
4. National Monument
5. Nelson's Memorial
6. Governor's House

Your walk starts here beside the memorial statue on the east (right-hand) side of the North Bridge which spans the valley which separated the original Old Town with the open farmlands to the north. The memorial statue was erected in 1906 to commemorate the soldiers of the King's Own Scottish Borderers who fell in the South African War.

Across the valley to your right, the prominent obelisk is the Martyrs' Monument. This is located in the Calton Burying Ground. The monument was erected in 1844 to commemorate a group of five Scottish political reformers who were persecuted for their democratic views during the French Revolutionary Wars at the end of the 18th century.

A View of the Calton Burial Ground

Most famous of these radicals was Thomas Muir a Glasgow lawyer. Muir was arrested and brought to trial in 1793. He defended himself but was mercilessly bullied by the trial judge, the notorious Lord Braxfield, who directed the jury to *"hang these damn scoundrels!"* Muir was found guilty of sedition and sentenced to fourteen years' transportation to Australia. On being given this savage sentence, Muir famously declared from the dock:

"Gentlemen, from my infancy to this moment I have devoted myself to the cause of the people. It is a good cause – it shall ultimately prevail – it shall finally triumph."

Thomas Muir

Muir and his fellow-accused were taken in chains to London and from there sent as convicts to Australia. In 1796 Muir was rescued from Botany Bay by friends in an American ship the *'Otter.'* After several adventures he was able to sail to safety in Revolutionary France. However his ship was intercepted by frigates of the Royal Navy off the coast of Spain in April 1797. Muir was badly wounded in the ensuing sea-battle; his left cheekbone was shot away and he was nearly blinded. He managed to reach France where he was greeted as a hero. Muir though died there of his wounds in 1799. Of the five who were convicted only one, Maurice Margarot, survived to return to Scotland at the end of his sentence in far-off Australia.

What looks like part of an old castle on the right is in fact the Governor's House of the former Calton Jail. This was opened in 1817 when the Tollbooth, the famous *'Heart of Midlothian'* the centuries-old jail in the High Street, was demolished.

The Calton Hill

The hill beyond is the Calton Hill, known as *'Edinburgh's Acropolis'*, which has several notable monuments. Prominent amongst these is the Nelson Monument, shaped like an upside-down telescope. This was built in 1816 to commemorate the famous sailor, Lord Nelson, who was killed at the Battle of Trafalgar fought in 1805.

There are also monuments to Robert Burns, Scotland's national poet and the philosopher Dugald Stewart, together with the City Observatory (1818) designed by the architect William Playfair and built in the style of a Greek Temple.

The most prominent monument however is the National Monument. This was planned as a war memorial to those Scottish soldiers and sailors who died during the long wars with France which only finished in 1815 with Napoleon's defeat at the Battle of Waterloo. The plan was to build a copy of the Parthenon in Athens. The foundation stone was laid in 1822. But money for the ambitious project soon ran out. The City of Edinburgh was bankrupted and in the end only twelve columns were completed. The National Monument then became known as *'Scotland's Folly and Edinburgh's Disgrace.'*

A walk up Calton Hill will show you the contrasting appearance of the Old and New Towns of Edinburgh. You will also get wonderful views across the Firth of Forth to Fife and to the Highlands beyond.

To your left runs Princes Street, the southern edge of Edinburgh's beautiful New Town. Some 250 years ago, just to the north of Princes Street, ran a country lane known as the *'Lang Dykes'*, (the long, stone walls). Behind lay open fields that ran northwards to the Firth of Forth broken only by a few scattered country houses, cottages and mills on the Water of Leith.

Register House c 1829

Register House is considered to be one of the finest classical buildings in Scotland. This was designed by Robert Adam, the well-known Scottish architect. Robert Adam was born in the Fife town of Kirkcaldy in 1728. His father William and brother James were both architects. Young Robert studied here in Edinburgh and then travelled to Italy. There he was very impressed by the ruins of Roman and Greek buildings.

For many years it had become fashionable both in Europe and what were then the American colonies, to have such classical features as columns and porticos built into stately homes and public buildings. (Both the White House and the American Congress building in Washington are good examples of this architectural fashion.) Robert Adam and his brother set up a business in London and became two of the most successful architects of their day.

For many years the historical records of Scotland had been gathering dust in a cellar underneath the old Parliament House in the Old Town of Edinburgh. Funds for the proposed Register House were provided by the government in London from the estates forfeited after the failed Jacobite Rebellion of 1745-46. The Town Council of Edinburgh granted land for a public building as they were anxious to encourage further development in their planned New Town. Work started in 1774 and was finally completed in 1784.

Adam's design incorporated special features to counteract the traditional enemies of archives - fire and damp. The building was solidly constructed of stone with brick vaults. Flues in the floor carried hot air from furnaces in the basement to protect the records from damp. Inside is the Adam Dome, a magnificent rotunda modelled on the Parthenon in Rome. An extension to the north, known as New Register House was completed in 1863.

Robert Adam

In front of Register House is a statue of the Duke of Wellington, the famous soldier who enjoyed the nickname of *'The Iron Duke'*. The statue was designed by Sir John Steell and cast in bronze. Wellington sat for the sculptor and was so pleased with the result that he ordered two additional copies for himself. The statue was unveiled on 18th June, 1852 during a violent thunderstorm. This prompted one Edinburgh wit to record that:

> *"Mid lightning's flash and thunder's deafening peal*
> *Behold the Iron Duke, in Bronze by Steell!"*

Looking back up towards the North Bridge, the building facing you used to be the Headquarters of the Post Office. This was built in Italian style and opened in 1866. It stood on the site of the former Shakespeare Square and the old Theatre Royal which were sadly demolished to make way for the Post Office development.

The Theatre Royal was opened in 1769. Many well-known actors performed here including Mrs Sarah Siddons, John Kemble and Edmund Kean. Mrs Siddons' first appearance on stage was met by silence from the Edinburgh audience which seriously disturbed the famous actress. She threw everything she had into her next scene to more silence and then a voice called out *"That's no' bad"* which provoked a storm of laughter and thunderous applause. When she was next due to appear there were 2,557 applications for 630 places and troops were required to quell the crush to get tickets. She was paid the staggering sum of £200 per night.

Perhaps the Theatre Royal's most memorable occasion was the performance of *'Rob Roy'* based on Sir Walter Scott's famous novel, on 27th August 1822 attended by King George IV during his famous visit to Edinburgh.

The Old Theatre Royal

The theatre was packed. People had been waiting since 1.00pm to get a seat. The dragoons had to be called in to control the crowds. The King arrived at 8.00pm. The play chosen was performed at the King's request. George was greeted with a roar and the whole cast took to the stage to sing the National Anthem. The King spent three hours at the theatre and enjoyed himself immensely. At his departure the National Anthem was sung again with a new verse added. George was overcome and wept.

> *Bright beams are soon o'ercast*
> *Soon our brief hour is past,*
> *Losing our King.*
> *Honoured, beloved and dear*
> *Still shall his parting ear*
> *Our latest accents hear*
> *God save the King.*

Across the road on the right is the Balmoral Hotel completed in 1902. It was built originally for the North British Railway Company and was known for years to Edinburgh folk as the NB Hotel. Its clock tower is one of the city's best-known landmarks. Traditionally the clock is kept two minutes fast to help travellers get to their trains on time in the neighbouring Waverley Station.

To your left is the entrance to Waterloo Place started in 1815 as a celebration of the end of the wars with France which ended at the Battle of Waterloo in June 1815. This was planned as an extension to the east of Princes Street. Regent Bridge, (named after the future George IV) carries the road past the Calton Burying Ground on the right towards the Calton Hill with its interesting monuments.

Now move to your right and take the first opening on your right. This leads you past the New Register House. Look out for a sign *'Gabriel's Road'*. This marks the start of an old country lane that used to run north-westwards through the open fields to Canonmills on the Water of Leith. Keep following Register Street as it bends to the left and continue towards St Andrew Square, past the famous Café Royal built in Parisian style and opened in 1863

There is an interesting story about the narrow street that you've just walked along. This was then known as St Andrews Lane and was the residence of the eccentric Edinburgh lawyer and historian, Hugo Arnot. He was one of the first well-to-do Edinburgh citizens who made the move from the Old Town. Hugo Arnot suffered badly from asthma and was painfully thin. He was rather eccentric and had rather a short temper as his neighbour found out in 1784. Arnot was in the habit of ringing a handbell very loudly when he wanted the attention of his servant.

This was too much for the lady who lived above him. She complained to him about his behaviour. He promised to stop using the bell. You can imagine her shock when next morning the peace was shattered by the sound of a pistol shot coming from Hugo Arnot's apartment. The lady raced down the stairs and opened the door to find Arnot sitting in his chair holding a smoking pistol.

"What on earth is going on?" she asked.

"Why Madam," replied Arnot. *"If I cannot ring my bell how else can I get my shaving water from my servant?*

Arnot was considered to be an excellent defence lawyer. However he only took on cases if he was convinced that his client was innocent. He deserves the credit for writing the first serious history of Edinburgh. In 1779, his *'History of Edinburgh'* was published. This is an excellent source of information about Scotland's capital. Sadly Arnot died on 30th November at the age of only 37.

Hugo Arnot (centre) arguing with Lord Monboddo

William Creech.

This was also where William Creech, the eminent publisher and later Lord Provost lived. Amongst other works, Creech publish the Edinburgh Edition of the poems of Robert Burns.

In 1789, a young lady called Miss Frances Burns moved into the house across the lane from his. She was by all accounts a stunning beauty. Miss Burns though enjoyed entertaining her gentlemen friends in her house, much to the annoyance of William Creech! He had Miss Burns brought before the Court demanding that she be banished from the city   Miss Burns though had plenty of admirers including Robert Burns, Scotland's national poet. In her defence he wrote:

> *"Cease ye prudes, your envious railing.*
> *Lovely Burns has charms – confess;*
> *True it is she had one failing –*
> *Had a woman ever less?"*

Frances Burns

The case was abandoned and Creech was ridiculed for his efforts. Miss Burns though decided that Edinburgh was too narrow-minded for a woman of her spirit. She moved to nearby Lasswade, where she died in 1792, aged only 23.

Now turn to your right and walk about 75 metres. Move into St Andrew Square and stop outside the impressive building at the eastern (right-hand) side with a statue in front of it. You are now standing in front of the building that was until recently the headquarters of the Royal Bank of Scotland. Some 250 years ago, you would have been in open countryside surrounded by fields and trees. Where the Royal Bank building now stands, was the *'Peace and Plenty Cottage'*. This was a popular stopping spot for Edinburgh folk out for a country walk. Here they would be served curds and cream, a popular treat of the day.

The Royal Bank was originally built as the town house of Sir Lawrence Dundas, a member of one of the most powerful families in late 18th century Scotland. He was a banker and a businessman who had made a fortune supplying the British Army in the Seven Years' War (1756 – 1763).

The former home of Sir Laurence Dundas

When Dundas learnt of the plans for the New Town he bought up the land where James Craig had intended the church of St Andrew to be built. To the dismay of the Town Council, Dundas proceeded to build this grand private house, modelled on Marble Hill House in London, in the popular classical style of architecture. It was rumoured at the time that Sir Laurence, who was a heavy gambler, lost his new home over a game of cards. Dundas though was so fond of his house that he paid for another house to be built for the man who had beaten him. Sir Lawrence died in 1781.

The building became the headquarters of the Royal Bank of Scotland in 1825 The statue in front of the Bank building is of Sir John Hope, 4th Earl of Hopetoun. Hope was a distinguished general during the long French wars and commanded the famous regiment, the 92nd Highlanders. The statue showing him as a Roman commander, was commissioned by the Town Council and unveiled in 1834.

Now turn round and have a look at St Andrew Square, named of course after the patron saint of Scotland. St Andrew Square, considered at one time to be one of the richest squares in Europe because of the concentration of banks and insurance companies, marks the eastern end of the original New Town of Edinburgh.

Amongst the first residents of the newly-completed square in 1778 were the Earls of Aboyne, Dumfries and Dalhousie.

The future Lord Henry Brougham was born in no. 21 in 1778. Brougham was to become a leading politician and served as Lord Chancellor from 1830 - 1834. He was one of the leaders of the campaign to abolish the Slave Trade. He was the designer of the Brougham, a four-wheeled, horse-drawn style of carriage that was named after him.

St Andrew Square c 1829

Here too lived Charles Gordon of Cluny in Aberdeenshire, one of Scotland's richest landowners. His beautiful daughter, Joanna was courted by their neighbour, John, the 7th Earl of Stair. The couple were married in 1804 but Joanna soon discovered that her husband was a thoroughly unpleasant man.

In 1808, the Earl of Stair abandoned Joanna and bigamously married another woman, Louise Manners. His crime though was discovered and this marriage was annulled. However Stair now made life even harder for the unfortunate Joanna. Eventually she managed to obtain a divorce in 1820. The strain though broke her health. She wasted away, suffered a complete mental breakdown and died here in 1847. As for the Earl of Stair, his unpopularity drove him from Edinburgh and he took refuge in Paris where he died in 1840. Stair had no children to succeed him, so the family name and title died with him.

St Andrew Square Gardens have been recently opened to the public and provide a welcome oasis in the busy New Town. In the Gardens stands the Melville Monument commemorating Henry Dundas, Viscount Melville, known as *the uncrowned King of Scotland* by his contemporaries.

Dundas ran Scotland for Prime Minister William Pitt at the end of the 18th century. An idea of just how unrepresentative Scottish politics were in those days can be gauged by the fact that only 25 people elected Edinburgh's one MP and in the election of 1790, Henry Dundas controlled 33 of the 45 Scottish seats. No wonder that he was nicknamed *King Harry the Ninth.*

A recent controversial development has been the decision by the City Council to add a plaque near to the monument accusing Dundas of postponing the abolition of slavery in the British Empire.

The Melville Monument

Dundas had served as Lord Advocate in Scotland but left the law following his election as MP for Midlothian in 1774. He was a great friend of William Pitt and held several important government positions including the Secretary of State for the Home Department and War Secretary during the first years of the French Revolutionary Wars. In 1804 he was appointed as First Lord of the Admiralty. In those days fraud and corruption in public life were commonplace. Dundas certainly used his position to better himself. However he made many political enemies who were jealous of his power.

They plotted to bring him down. In 1805 he was accused before the House of Lords of mishandling funds whilst acting as Treasurer of the Royal Navy.

However, after a trial lasting two weeks, he was cleared of all charges. His political life though was finished. He retired to his estate in Comrie, Perthshire and died in 1811.

Henry Dundas (on the left)

The monument, which was designed by the well-known Edinburgh architect William Burn, was erected in 1820. The monument, which stands 42.6 metres high (140 feet), proved to be extremely challenging to complete. Robert Stevenson the famous lighthouse engineer and grandfather of the well-known Edinburgh author Robert Louis Stevenson, was brought in to assist. He used the crane that had helped construct the Bell Lighthouse to put the monument in place.

The statue of Dundas, sculpted by Sir Francis Chantrey, was added in 1823. A plaque records that the cost of £8000 was voluntarily subscribed by the officers and men of the Royal Navy. You have to wonder though what choice the ordinary seamen had in supporting the project!

Dr Alexander Wood (1725 – 1802) was another of the early residents of this part of the New Town. Unlike many of his landowning neighbours, he had to work to earn his living.

He was a practicing doctor who made the journey each working day on foot up to his patients in the Old Town. He was a tall, thin man who was nicknamed *'Lang Sandy Wood'*.

Dr Alexander Wood

He was much-loved and would go out of his way to help his patients. He was credited with being the first person in Edinburgh to own an umbrella which you can see tucked under his arm as he makes his way over the North Bridge.

For many years he lived in nearby York Place where he kept a pet sheep and a raven. The sheep watched out for its master from behind the railings in front of the Royal Bank where it grazed while the raven perched on a nearby tree.

The Scottish National Portrait Gallery

Now retrace your steps and continue down to Queen Street. The prominent red sandstone building is the Scottish National Portrait Gallery. The building, which is decorated with statues of figures from Scottish History, was built between 1885-1890 to house The Portrait Gallery and the National Museum of Scottish Antiquities. The building was funded by a gift of £50000 by John Ritchie Findlay, the owner of *'The Scotsman'* newspaper.

John Ritchie Findlay

One of the most prominent features of the Gallery is the William Hole Mural which decorates the walls of the central hall. The colourful mural shows over 150 prominent historical Scots together with larger paintings of dramatic scenes from Scotland's history including the Battle of Bannockburn at which King Robert Bruce's army defeated the much larger forces of King Edward II of England in June 1314 to secure Scotland's independence.

The Gallery's collection totals some 3,000 paintings and sculptures together with 25,000 prints and drawings. Portraits of many famous Scots are on display including Mary, Queen of Scots, David Hume, Flora Macdonald, Robert Burns and Sir Walter Scott. There are also portraits of modern Scots such as Sir Alex Ferguson, Jean Redpath, John Byrne and Billy Connolly.

Regular themed exhibitions are held. In addition to its collection of portraits, the Gallery holds the Scottish National Photography Collection. This includes the pioneering work of David Octavius Hill and Robert Adamson whose calotypes date from the 1840s. Their pioneering work here in Edinburgh saw the start of photography in Scotland. You will learn about the event which saw Hill and Adamson turn to photography on p. 36.

The gallery reopened on 1 December 2011 after being closed since April 2009 for the first comprehensive refurbishment in its history. It now forms part of the National Galleries of Scotland. Admission is free and there is a very good café.

3. THISTLE COURT TO THE MOUND

George Street and St Andrews Church c 1829

MAP 2

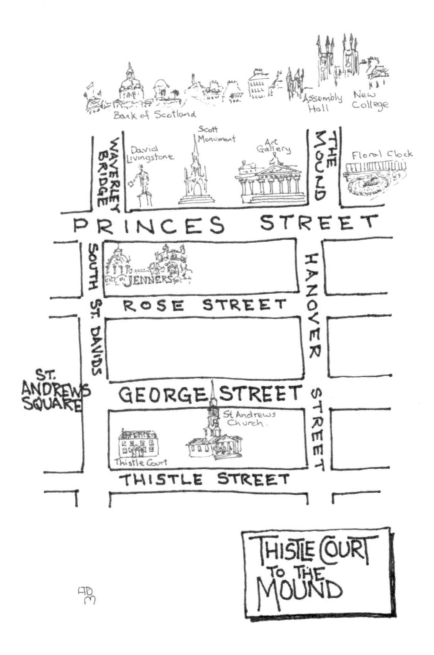

Now walk back up North St David's Street and turn right into Thistle Street. A few paces will bring you to Thistle Court. The little house on the left of the Court is in fact the first house to be built in the New Town. It was built in 1767 for John Young and the foundation stone was laid by James Craig. Young was awarded £20 by the Town Council for being the first to make his home in the New Town.

As you can see, it is a rather modest building and certainly not what the Town Council had wanted to see in their grand New Town! So regulations were introduced to ensure that every house that was to be built on the main streets was to be built of dressed ashlar stone; have three stories and a sunken basement; have its own entrance and a street frontage of no more than 48 feet (14.4metres).

No.1 Thistle Court (left-hand door). The first house built in the New Town

Now make your way up to the start of George Street. This was planned as the principal street of the New Town. The width of the street, which so impressed visitors, was designed to allow two carriages to turn safely without bumping into each other.

Take a moment to look along the length of what was designed as the most important street in the New Town (after all it was named after the King!). To your right, you can see the distant dome and spire of what was originally St George's Church (now West Register House) in Charlotte Square.

Having started as a residential street, by the late 1800s over thirty different insurance companies had their offices here. George Street now is the home to several of Edinburgh's most fashionable shops, restaurants and bars.

Looking west along George Street

Professor James Clark Maxwell

At the east end of George Street is the statue of the Scottish physicist and mathematician James Clark Maxwell (1831 – 1879).   He is perhaps best known for his work in electromagnetics and quantum physics. In 1861 he produced the world's first permanent colour photograph.   His work paved the way for the digital age. In the millennium poll – a survey of the 100 most prominent physicists – Maxwell was voted the third greatest physicist of all time, behind only Newton and Einstein.

What about St Andrew's Church? This was the first church to be built in the New Town. The architect was a retired military officer, Major Andrew Fraser. Work started in 1785. The beautiful oval-shaped church has many classical features, a fine portico and a peal of eight bells – the oldest in Scotland. This church of course should have been built in St Andrew Square! The church was the scene of the famous disruption of the Church of Scotland in 1843.

St Andrew's Church

The General Assembly of the Church of Scotland had gathered here for the annual meeting of ministers and elders from all over Scotland. The church spilt in two over the question of who should have the responsibility for appointing new ministers – should it be the congregation or the rich landowners?

Watched by thousands who had packed George Street, 470 ministers and elders walked out of the meeting and marched down Hanover Street to the nearby Tanfield Hall at Canonmills where they founded the Free Church of Scotland. In time the Free Church itself was split but the original Free Church reunited with the Church of Scotland and the first General Assembly of the reunited Church of Scotland was held here in St. Andrew's Church in 1929.

The leaders of the new Free Church of Scotland wished to have the historic first meeting of their General Assembly in Tanfield Hall to be recorded for posterity in a painting. They turned to David Octavius Hill, at that time one of Scotland best-known artists. There was though a real challenge for Hill. How was he to gather accurate likenesses of all those involved?

Hill was helped by his young friend Robert Adamson, a chemist, who had just been introduced to the new Calotype photography. They opened a studio in Edinburgh and invited the leaders of the Free Church to come to be photographed. They soon realised the potential of photography and took some of the first landscape photos ever taken. Sadly their partnership ended in 1848 with Adamson's untimely death.

David Octavius Hill c 1845

The Dome decorated for Christmas

Across the road from St Andrew's Church is the imposing building known as The Dome. This is now a popular bar and restaurant in Edinburgh's New Town. It is famous for its colourful decorations put up to celebrate the festive season. The interior is stunning and is well worth a visit.

The Interior of the Dome

The building dates from 1847 when it was built for the Commercial Bank of Scotland. It replaced an earlier building, the Physician's Hall built for the Royal College of Physicians in the 1770s. This was in fact the only building actually designed by James Craig, the winner of the competition to design the New Town. This was his only successful commission for this phase of the growth of Edinburgh to the north. However the building was deemed to be very unattractive and so it was demolished.

Now cross over to South St David's Street. How did St David's Street get its name? The obvious answer is that the street was named after St David, the patron saint of Wales. There is however another answer which pokes friendly fun at one of the street's first residents, David Hume, the famous historian, diplomat and philosopher. In 1741 Hume published the very-popular *'Essays Moral and Political'* and amongst other books, his five volume *'History of England'* established his reputation as an author of international standing. Between 1763 – 1765 he worked as Secretary to the British Ambassador in Paris. Here he was welcomed into French literary and academic circles. He wrote to a friend:

"Here I feed on ambrosia, drink nothing but nectar, breathe incense only and walk on flowers

In 1768 he returned to Edinburgh where he became the centre of the town's literary and academic circle. This was the time when Edinburgh shone as the intellectual capital of Europe. Amongst Hume's glittering circle of friends were Adam Smith, the economist; William Robertson the fellow-historian, Joseph Black the physicist; William Cullen the chemist and James Hutton, the father of modern geology. With his rational approach to knowledge, Hume was very much their inspiration.

David Hume

Despite his obvious talents, Hume was turned down for a professorship at Edinburgh University. Why was this? Well we must remember that in those days any holder of public office in Scotland had to be a practicing Christian of the Presbyterian faith. David Hume did not believe in God. So an academic post was denied him. Nevertheless his genius was recognised by his contemporaries. He corresponded with leading international intellectual figures and delighted in debating contemporary issues at the meetings of the Philosophical Society, now the Royal Society of Edinburgh.

What about the street name? Well, the story is that when David Hume first moved into his new house, the street had not been named. Knowing Hume's reputation as an atheist, the daughter of one of his new neighbours, chalked 'St David's Street' on the wall outside his house – and the name stuck. Surrounded by friends, Hume died here in 1776. He is buried in the near-by Calton Burial Ground.

Another story of David Hume tells of how he was keen to see the progress being made with his new home in the New Town. With the North Bridge being repaired, Hume left his Old Town apartment in James Court and took a short-cut across the partially-drained Nor' Loch. Hume slipped and fell in.

Hume was rather heavily-built and struggled to get out. He had to be pulled free of the mud by two Newhaven fishwives who would only help him if he would recite The Lord's Prayer – which he did.

A Newhaven Fishwife

David Hume can be very much seen as the trailblazer for the intellectual flowering of Edinburgh in the second half of the 18th century. Observers were conscious that this was truly a *'Golden Age'* for Edinburgh.

"Today it is from Scotland that we get rules of taste in all the arts from epic poetry to gardening." (Voltaire 1762).

"More true learning is to be found in Edinburgh than in Oxford and Cambridge taken together." (J.W. von Archenholz 1780)

"Taken altogether I do not know any other town, where it would be pleasanter to live. It is in a great degree the Geneva of Britain." (Louis Simond 1815).

The original proposals of 1752 had assumed that it would only be *"People of fortune and of a certain rank"* who would move to the New Town as *"men of professions and business of every kind will still incline to live in the neighbourhood of the Exchange, of the Courts of Justice and other places of public resort* (in the Old Town)." Soon though professional families were also making the move to the growing New Town.

When the silk merchant John Neale built the first house at the east end of Princes Street in 1769, he was exempted from city taxes for life. Gradually leading citizens like David Hume were persuaded to set up home in the developing New Town. Despite the inconvenience of access and initially the lack of any shops, the attraction of these spacious houses proved to be irresistible. And no wonder! With their own private entrance, (compared to the common tenement stair of the Old Town), drawing room, dining room, study, bedrooms, kitchen and ample space for servants and storage, these houses soon attracted buyers. Indeed the first New Town proved to be so popular that other residential developments quickly followed.

A View from the East End of Princes Street c 1829

While the original plan had thought of George Street as the principal street of the New Town, it was Princes Street that quickly proved to be the most popular – and a glance up towards the Royal Mile will tell you why. An early attempt to build houses on the south side of Princes Street was rejected by the Town Council. Their decision was upheld by the House of Lords in London in 1774 and so this majestic view up to Edinburgh Castle and the Old Town remains.

Now cross over Princes Street and look back towards the famous Jenners, Scotland's oldest and grandest Department Store. Jenners was started in 1838 by Charles Jenner and Charles Kennington. The original store was burnt down in 1892 and replaced by the present building which is modelled on a Renaissance palace. The business remained in the hands of the Douglas-Miller family, descendants of Charles Kennington, until 2005 when it was sold to House of Fraser.

Jenners Department Store

Now turn to look at the familiar landmark of the Scott Monument. Work started on this memorial to the great Scottish writer Sir Walter Scott in 1840. We will learn more about Scott, further on in our walk.

The Scott Monument

The much-loved author had died in 1832. Such was his fame that it was decided that it would be appropriate for a memorial to be built on the south side of Princes Street. A competition was held and architects were invited to submit plans for a suitable memorial to *'The Wizard of the North.'*

 The winner was George Meikle Kemp, a carpenter by trade, from the Scottish Borders – not an architect. Kemp was though a very talented architectural draughtsman. He had modestly submitted his competition entry under a pseudonym – *'John Morvo'* who had been a 16th century master mason at Melrose Abbey. His design in the newly-fashionable Gothic style, drew heavily from the ruins of Melrose Abbey in the Scottish Borders, close to Scott's home of Abbotsford.

George Meikle Kemp
(Calotype by David Octavius Hill)

The monument is 200 feet (61 metres) high and is the tallest monument to a writer in the world. It is decorated with figures from Scott's writing. The statue of Scott with his favourite dog Maida was by Sir John Steell. Sadly Kemp did not live to see the completion of his work. He was found drowned in the Union Canal in 1844. Possibly he had lost his footing one foggy night when he had gone to check on the arrival of a barge carrying stone for the monument. It is well-worth the climb up the monument's 287 steps for the views of the city from the top platform.

The partially-built Scott Monument c 1845

Next to the Scott Monument is a statue of David Livingstone, the celebrated Scottish explorer and missionary. Livingstone was born in Blantyre in Lanarkshire. His family were very poor and from the ages of 10 to 24 he worked in a cotton mill. He then trained as a medical missionary and dedicated the rest of his life to exploring the interior of Central Africa. He was the first European to reach the Victoria Falls and Lake Nyasa. He campaigned hard against the cruelty of the slave trade that he witnessed. His wife, who accompanied him, died in Africa in 1862 and for several years there was no news of Dr. Livingstone.

The American newspaper 'The New York Herald' commissioned the Welsh-born adventurer Henry Morton Stanley to go in search of Livingstone. After many dangers and hardships, Stanley found Livingstone at the village of Ujiji in 1871. He tried to persuade Livingstone to return home with him but Livingstone was determined to carry on with his work. Livingstone died in present-day Zambia in 1873. His faithful servants embalmed his body and carried it to the East African coast. From there it was brought to London. Livingstone was buried in Westminster Abbey.

Dr. David Livingstone

Now make your way about 100 metres westwards along this the south side of Princes Street and pause in the pedestrian area facing the two art galleries that are in front of you at the foot of The Mound.

You can see in these buildings, clear evidence of the strong classical influence on the architecture of New Town Edinburgh. Work started on the first building, the Royal Institution, (now the Royal Scottish Academy), in 1822. The building is modelled on a Greek Doric temple. The statue of a seated Queen Victoria by Sir John Steell, was added in 1844. The architect was William Playfair, who over the course of a career spanning some 50 years was responsible for designing many of Edinburgh's best-known buildings. The Royal Scottish Academy now has a permanent art collection. There are also regular themed exhibitions.

The National Gallery of Scotland

The National Gallery of Scotland on your left was started in 1845. The architect was also William Playfair. Again you can see the strong influence of Greece with its Corinthian columns and Ionic porticos.

The National Gallery, which has recently been extended, has one of the finest collections in Britain of European Art from the 15th to the 19th centuries. The National Gallery includes works by such well-known artists as Raphael, Titian, Rembrandt, Rubens, Reynolds and Gainsborough. A gallery is dedicated to Scottish painting where you can see work by Sir Henry Raeburn, Allan Ramsay, David Allan, Elizabeth Blackadder and John Bellany amongst others.

And what of The Mound itself? It certainly was not planned by James Craig. It just appeared as the result of the builders of the New Town simply dumping the excavated soil and stones from the foundations of the houses and gardens being built as the New Town progressed westwards.

'Geordie Boyd's Mud Brig' – a contemporary cartoon

In 1781, George Boyd, a clothier living in Gosford's Close in the Old Town, put down planks on the Mound to make it easier for him to reach his New Town customers. For a while the Mound was nick-named *'Geordie Boyd's Mud Brig.'* This contemporary cartoon by John Kay, the famous caricaturist, shows George Boyd as a coachman driving a team of his fellow-tradesmen from the Old Town on a coach down the *'Mud Brig'* to the New Town. He was followed by Lord Provost John Grieve who had bought a new house on the corner of Hanover Street and Princes Street. It has been suggested that it was John Grieve who was responsible for the Mound being aligned with his front door rather than with the adjacent Hanover Street. Soon the Mound became a popular, if at times muddy, causeway.

A View from the top of the Mound c 1829

This 1829 view from the top of The Mound clearly shows different tracks crossing the dumped builders' spoil. It also shows the recently completed Royal Institution (now the Royal Scottish Academy), the spire of St Andrew's Church in George Street and the Melville Monument in St Andrew Square. Note the clean stonework of the New Town houses.

The original plan of James Craig for this New Town had proposed the draining of the Nor' Loch which by the 1760s was little better than an open sewer. Once drained, there was to be a canal built in the valley that separated the Old Town from the New. This dream was now lost forever.

Many contemporaries were outraged. Lord Henry Cockburn a senior judge and early conservationist wrote:

"One of the greatest mistakes committed as a matter of taste was the erection of the Earthen Mound across the beautiful valley of the loch."

There was no going back however and in 1834 The Mound was paved and lit. When the Edinburgh and Glasgow Railway was extended to Waverley in 1846, tunnels were driven under The Mound to allow access to the west.

The Christmas Torchlight Procession on The Mound

Princes Street has certainly seen some excitement in its time. There have been royal processions and military parades; cavalcades, protest marches and demonstrations.

Each September, the streets and the Gardens behind you are packed with spectators to see the spectacular Fireworks Concert that traditionally ends the Edinburgh International Festival. Edinburgh's Hogmanay is world-famous. On December 31st, thousands of revellers from all over the world pack into Princes Street to celebrate the arrival of the New Year with music and another fireworks' display against the unbeatable backdrop of Edinburgh Castle.

Before we leave the foot of the Mound, cross over the road and enter this section of Princes Street Gardens. There you will see Edinburgh's colourful mechanical Floral Clock. The Clock, the first such clock in the world, was created in 1903 by John McHattie of the City Parks' Department. A new design is planted each year using some 35,000 plants. They used to be planted separately but now are planted in specially-designed containers. The statue above is of Allan Ramsay, the 18th century Scottish poet, whose equally famous son, also Allan, was a well-known artist.

The Floral Clock

Successive commercial developments have meant that there is very little of the original housing still to be seen in this section of Princes Street. However if you look closely above the shop fronts, you can still occasionally see something of the former houses. There is more to be seen as you progress westwards.

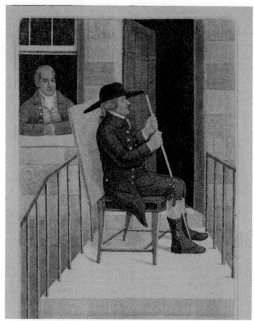

Robert Craig of Riccarton c 1788

This charming caricature by John Kay shows Robert Craig of Riccarton sitting outside his house, No. 91 Princes Street, enjoying the early morning sun. This is a reminder that the New Town was originally planned for residential development only. However the inconvenience for householders of having to go, or more likely having to send their servants, back up to the Old Town for their provisions soon saw the ground floor properties in Princes Street converted into shops.

If you look to the top of The Mound you will see on the left, the impressive bulk of the headquarters of The Bank of Scotland founded in 1695. Work started on the Bank's headquarters in 1802 and it was extensively rebuilt in the 1860s. The bank houses a fascinating (and free) museum. Here visitors can find out something of the Bank's colourful history. Amongst the exhibits is the first chest, or 'kist' dating from the start of the 18th century where the bank's cash was kept. Another section of the Museum tells the story of what has been used as money in the past with examples from around the world such as shells, tea and even feathers. You can also try to break open a safe.

The tall building on the right above the grass is New College opened in 1850 originally as a teaching college for the Free Church of Scotland. Behind it through a courtyard is the Assembly Hall built in 1859 as the meeting place for the General Assembly of the Church of Scotland. It is also a very popular location for theatrical productions during the annual Edinburgh International Festival.

The Bank of Scotland

A View of Princes Street c 1823

This fascinating view by the Scottish artist Alexander Nasmyth, looks east along Princes Street towards the Calton Hill and the North Bridge. You can see clearly the contrast between the straight, regular buildings of the New Town with the skyline of the historic Old Town.

The ridge on the right is the accumulated builders' spoil from work done in and around St Andrew Square that had been dumped in the partially-drained Nor' Loch. This is now Waverley Bridge. You can also see on the right the recently completed Bank of Scotland building standing at the top of what is now Bank Street. The painting shows work underway at the Royal Institution at the foot of the Mound. (Now the Royal Scottish Academy.) Already there are some shops to be seen on Princes Street. Quite clearly though there are no traffic regulations to be followed.

4. FROM HANOVER STREET TO QUEEN STREET

The Assembly Rooms, George Street c 1829

MAP 3

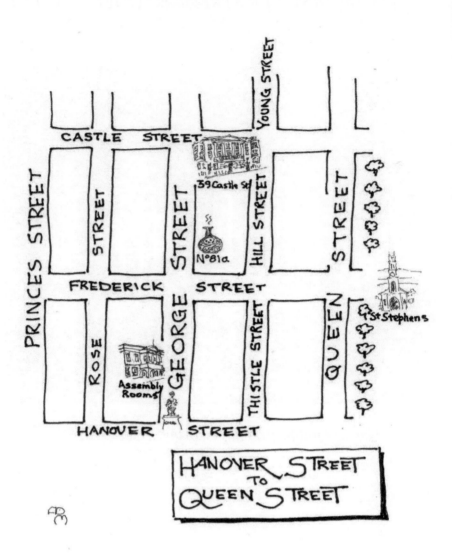

CASTLE STREET

PRINCES STREET

STREET

GEORGE STREET

39 Castle St

N°81a

YOUNG STREET

HILL STREET

QUEEN STREET

FREDERICK STREET

ROSE

Assembly Rooms

THISTLE STREET

† St Stephens

HANOVER STREET

HANOVER STREET
TO
QUEEN STREET

Cross over Princes Street and make your way up Hanover Street towards the crossing with George Street. Here you will see much more evidence of the original New Town houses of the 1780s. Sir Francis Chantrey's statue of George IV was erected in 1831 to celebrate the King's famous visit to Edinburgh in August 1822.

It has to be said that the statue is very flattering! King George was by then 58 years old and years of over-eating and heavy drinking had left him very overweight. Although standing only about 5' 2" (160 cms), George weighed nearly 19 stone (120 kgs) and his waist in 1795 was measured at 51" (130 cms)! No wonder that Sir Walter Scott privately referred to George as *"our fat friend."*

George IV

The visit of King George was eagerly anticipated. It had been some 200 years since a monarch had last visited Edinburgh. The visit was organised by Sir Walter Scott. He planned it to be a celebration of all things Scottish – particularly the traditional clan-life of the Highlands.

Quite clearly the expectation was that tartan was to be the order of the day. Those attending the planned Balls for the King were advised that:

"No gentleman is to be allowed to appear in anything but the ancient Highland costume."

Virtually single-handedly, Scott had created the modern Scottish tourist industry with its iconic images of tartan, bagpipes, Scottish Country Dancing and of course, whisky.

Thousands of people poured into Edinburgh from all over Scotland. Many of them camped in the King's Park at the foot of Arthur's Seat. The Royal Yacht anchored at Leith on August 15th 1822. The King was driven in a carriage past cheering crowds up Leith Walk, through St Andrew Square and along Princes Street to Holyrood Palace.

The Royal Procession of George IV beneath Calton Hill

For two weeks the King was entertained in his royal capital. He visited the Castle and Holyrood Palace, worshipped at St Giles Kirk, attended the Theatre Royal, knighted Henry Raeburn the artist and took the salute at a Parade of the Clans. A magnificent banquet in his honour was held in Parliament Hall. King George even appeared in public wearing a kilt in the Royal Stewart tartan, complimented by pink silk tights. This caused much amusement as the King's kilt was rather short which prompted Lady Hamilton - Dalrymple to remark:

"Since his stay was so short, the more we see of him the better."

A contemporary cartoon makes fun of George IV's short kilt

Thanks though to Sir Walter Scott, the Royal Visit of 1822 was a resounding success.

Now move along George Street to the Assembly Rooms. For better-off Edinburgh folk, the Assembly was one of the highlights of their winter social calendar. This was a weekly dance started at the end of the 17th century. These popular assemblies were held in the Old Assembly Close and then from 1756 in the New Assembly Rooms in Bell's Wynd off the High Street.

Clearly for those young people whose families had moved to the New Town, it was far too much trouble to travel all the way back up to the High Street, so money was raised and new Assembly Rooms were planned for George Street. The building was designed by John Henderson and work started in 1784. The portico was added in 1818. A Music Hall was added to the rear of the Assembly Rooms in 1843 designed by William Burn.

The Assembly Rooms c 1829

Try to imagine the scene with carriages drawing up at the door and beautifully-dressed young ladies being escorted into the building by servants carrying torches. It would appear though that the ladies usually had to wait for their male escorts to arrive – often the worse for wear!

Here is how one contemporary, Hugo Arnot, described the scene:

"Gentlemen reeling from the tavern flustered with wine stumbled into an assembly of as elegant and beautiful women as any in Europe."

The Assembly Rooms were also the setting for the two Highland Balls held to honour King George IV during his famous visit in August 1822. Although too overweight to dance, the King sat on a raised chair and clapped his hands in delight as the tartan-clad guests danced a programme of Strathspeys and Reels to the music of Nathaniel Gow, son of the celebrated Scottish fiddler Niel Gow. Many of the tunes composed by the Gows are still danced today.

It was here in the Assembly Rooms at a dinner arranged in his honour in 1827, that Sir Walter Scott first publicly acknowledged that he was indeed the author of the popular *Waverley Novels* which included such tales as 'The Heart of Midlothian', 'Rob Roy' and 'Ivanhoe'. These historical novels brought Scott immense fame and wealth. He was the most widely-read author of the 19th century and is credited with inventing the modern historical novel.

Here too other popular authors of the day would give readings from their books. Charles Dickens made several visits. On one occasion though in 1861, the organisers had issued too many tickets and the hall where Dickens was to read from his ever-popular story 'A Christmas Carol', was packed to overflowing. Several people fainted and many were crushed, but undeterred Dickens completed his reading to thunderous applause.

The Assembly Rooms' Ballroom

There is another story, or at least an Edinburgh legend, about the Assembly Rooms which links Charles Dickens and *'A Christmas Carol'* with the visit of George IV in 1822. It is said that to take charge of the catering planned for the Royal Visit, Sir Walter Scott turned to an Edinburgh merchant Ebenezer Scroggie.

He had been born in Kirkcaldy and was a cousin of economist Adam Smith. Scroggie became a successful merchant, vintner and Town Councillor in Edinburgh. He held the first contract to supply whisky to the Royal Navy in Leith. Scroggie was known as a dandy and something of a ladies' man which made him the talk of the town. He was a jovial and kindly man, not the mean-spirited miser with whom he was to become associated. So how did this happen? It can all be traced apparently to a mistake on a gloomy late afternoon in an Edinburgh kirkyard.

The error, it is claimed, came about when author Charles Dickens was walking in Edinburgh after a public reading of his work in the early 1840s. He explored the Canongate Kirkyard in the Old Town and noted Scroggie's memorial stone. This described Ebenezer Scroggie as a '*meal man*', that is a corn dealer. Due to the fading light and his mild dyslexia, Dickens mis-read this as a '*mean man*' The famous author was shocked. He supposedly later wrote in his notebook :

"To be remembered through eternity only for being mean seemed the greatest testament to a life wasted." (It must have) *"shrivelled his* (Scroggie's) *soul to carry such a terrible thing to eternity"*.

Thus the character Ebenezer Scrooge supposedly came into being in '*A Christmas Carol*', first published in 1843, and Scroggie forever acquired an ill-deserved reputation. It is claimed that the grave marker was lost during construction work in part of the kirkyard in 1932. There is though no hard evidence from the official census that Scroggie ever existed! A great story if it is true but…??

Another early visitor to Edinburgh's New Town was Vincent Lunardi. The famous Italian balloonist came to Edinburgh in 1785 and stayed in Walker's Hotel in Princes Street. On 5th October of that year he made a balloon ascent from the grounds of Heriot's Hospital. A crowd of 80,000 gathered to witness the event. At noon a flag was raised from Edinburgh Castle and a gun was fired at the scene.

The balloon was inflated and at 2.45pm rose into the air. The wind took Lunardi out over the Forth and past Inchkeith. From there he was carried eastwards over North Berwick and then across the Firth to land in a field near Ceres in Fife. The local minister, the Rev. Arnot, had to rescue him from a crowd of terrified farm workers.

He was feted with a dinner in Cupar and next day honoured in St Andrews. He made four other flights in Scotland including another in Edinburgh. He was very full of himself and boasted of his reputation with the young ladies of Edinburgh. He once toasted himself thus *'Lunardi, whom the ladies love'*. The Lunardi Bonnet became fashionable for ladies and is mentioned by Burns in his poem *'Tae a Louse'*. He died in Italy in 1809.

Vincent Lunardi in Edinburgh

The dream of the Town Council was that the planned New Town with its grand houses would prove to be very attractive to the better-off citizens of Edinburgh.

At first though there was a great reluctance on the part of Edinburgh folk to leave the familiar surroundings of the Old Town and to take up residence in what after all was a large building site surrounded by fields. And it was to be a building site for nearly 60 years!

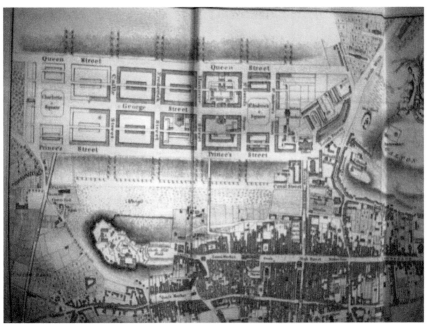

The New Town's progress – a plan of the 1780s

Work proceeded very slowly from east to west. Hanover Street was started in 1784; Frederick Street in 1786 and Castle Street in 1792. Charlotte Square, started in 1792, was not completed until 1811. Even before James Craig's New Town was completed, further building works were taking place that were to extend the New Town yet further. In all six other projects were started including the development of the Heriot Estate to the north of Queen Street and the Moray Estate to the west of Charlotte Square started in 1822.

Continue west along George Street. No. 81a was the home of Eugene – Marie Chantrelle who was hanged in 1878 for poisoning his young wife Elizabeth Dyer. Chantrelle had come to Edinburgh to take up a position as a French teacher. He was forced to marry one of his students, 17 years' old Elizabeth Dyer when she became pregnant. The marriage was not a happy one.

Eugene – Marie Chantrelle

In October 1877, Chantrelle took out a life insurance policy for his wife for £1,000. On New Year's Day 1878 a maid found Elizabeth lying dead in bed in their house here in George Street.

At first it was thought that her death had been caused by a broken gas pipe found under the bed. However, Dr Henry Littlejohn, Edinburgh's Medical Officer of Health, was very suspicious. He asked for a further post-mortem to be carried out. Traces of opium were found in Elizabeth's body. Chantrelle was arrested and charged with the murder of his wife. He was found guilty and sentenced to be hanged. The execution took place at the Calton Gaol on 31st May 1878. Chantrelle's execution was the first to be carried out in private in Edinburgh.

Now turn back and go down Frederick Street. Ahead of you is St Stephen's Church. It was built in 1827 to a design by William Playfair.

The Edinburgh tradition is that the church was placed here quite deliberately by the Town Council to hide the recently-completed Edinburgh Academy, tucked behind it in Henderson Row. The Council was angry that this independent school had been set up in competition to the burgh's High School. The Academy had been promoted by several leading Edinburgh citizens including Sir Walter Scott and Lord Cockburn who felt that the standard of classics' teaching at the High School was not good enough for young Scots seeking employment in England where they were competing with the products of the English public schools.

St Stephen's Church

Work started on Frederick Street in 1786. The street was named after Frederick, the Duke of York, second son of George III. As mentioned previously, he is perhaps better known as the incompetent general of the popular children's nursery rhyme *'The Grand Old Duke of York'*.

As you walk down Frederick Street, you will cross Thistle Street. This narrow lane was, like Rose Street, originally intended as a more modest street with homes for shopkeepers, servants and tradesmen. There was also stabling. However, such was the desire to obtain a house in the expanding (and increasingly expensive!) New Town, that the houses were soon taken over by professional people and even people of rank.

Amongst the more colourful of the earlier residents were Charles Edward Stuart, the self-styled Count of Albany and his brother who called himself John Sobieski Stuart.

John Sobieski Stuart (John Allan)

They claimed to be the grand-sons of Bonnie Prince Charlie, the exiled leader of the Jacobite cause who had been defeated at the Battle of Culloden in April 1746. They dressed extravagantly in Highland costume and were welcomed into society. In fact though, they were imposters. Far from being members of the Royal Stuart family, they were born in Wales, the sons of Captain Thomas Allan of the Royal Navy. The brothers spent much time in the Highlands and wrote several books to back up their claims and to promote ancient Scottish history. Both their claims and their writings were challenged though and the brothers felt obliged to leave Scotland. They are though both buried in the Highlands at Eskadale not far from Inverness.

Behind the remaining original houses you can still see some of the surviving stables - a reminder that the New Town was built in the age of horses and carriages. Thistle Street continues westwards first as Hill Street and then as Young Street, the names of the two builders James Hill and John Young who developed each section.

Original Stabling for the Moray Estate

Turn left and make your way along Queen Street. Look at the buildings around you. Here you will find a greater concentration of the original 18th century houses of the first New Town. The gardens to the north of you belong to the residents and were laid out in 1823. It is perhaps hard to appreciate that when the first residents moved into these houses, they had open country behind them running down to the Firth of Forth beyond. Writing in 1824, William Chambers, the well-known Edinburgh writer and publisher, remarked that:

"Many are still alive (who) remember the fields bearing a rich crop of wheat that now bear houses. Game used to be plentiful on these grounds, in particular partridge and hares."

No. 52 Queen Street

Perhaps the most famous early resident of Queen Street was Sir James Young Simpson who lived for many years at No. 52. It was here on the night of 28th November 1847 that he and two medical friends, Drs. Keith and Duncan, discovered the anaesthetic properties of chloroform.

The search for a means of overcoming the pain of surgery and of childbirth had for years challenged the medical profession. On that night in 1847, Simpson and his friends inhaled chloroform from individual glasses and napkins. The next thing that Dr Simpson remembered was finding himself on the floor with his friends snoring beside him.

Dr Simpson was hailed as a saviour throughout the medical world. Honours were showered upon him but he continued in a typically modest way to carry out his work as a doctor. Queen Victoria had chloroform for the birth of her seventh child Prince Leopold, the Duke of Albany in 1853.

Dr. Simpson died in November 1870. A grateful nation offered his family a tomb in Westminster Abbey in London. This honour was declined and he is buried in nearby Warriston Cemetery. His funeral was attended by 1,700 men in deep mourning and the procession was watched by a crowd of some 10,0000 people, many of them in tears.

Dr James Young Simpson

Before continuing your tour, look over Queen Street Gardens towards the north. The original householders had a clear view over the Firth of Forth towards Fife and the Highland mountains beyond. This view was interrupted in 1807 when work started on an extension to the New Town.

The governors of George Heriot's Hospital (now George Heriot's School) sold land that they held for residential development. Again the idea was for a series of parallel streets running from Heriot Row in the south to Fettes Row in the north. The connecting streets with Hanover Street and Frederick Street were named after leading figures and places of the day such as Prime Minister Pitt, Henry Dundas, Viscount Melville, Admiral Richard Howe and Cape St Vincent, scene of a famous naval victory over the French in 1797. This development was completed to the west by the construction of the Royal Circus in 1823. In the meantime a further extension was started to the west with the development of the adjacent Moray Estate in the 1820s for residential housing.

Moray Place

These were houses on a grand scale designed by the architect Gillespie Graham. He took the inspiration of Royal Circus to create three sweeping curves, Randolph Crescent, Ainslie Place and the grandest of them all, the 12-sided Moray Place. The developer, the 10th Earl of Moray who stayed in No. 28, chose family names for these streets.

Now turn left and walk to the junction with Castle Street. Turn left again and walk back up towards Princes Street. The street takes its name from the magnificent views up towards Edinburgh Castle. Kenneth Grahame, the author of the much-loved children's story *'The Wind in the Willows'* was born in house No. 30. Just round the corner in Young Street is the Oxford Bar, the favourite pub of John Rebus, the famous Edinburgh detective created by author Ian Rankin.

Stop in front of No. 39. This was the home for many years of Sir Walter Scott.

No. 39 Castle Street

Sir Walter Scott lived here from 1800 to 1826. Much of his best work was written in the study of this house. Scott has already made a couple of appearances during our tour. Although not as widely-read as he once was, Scott dominated 19th century British literature. As most of his stories and poems were set in Scotland it is not surprising that he was nicknamed *'The Wizard of the North'*.

Scott was born in Edinburgh's Old Town in College Wynd in 1771. His father was a successful Edinburgh lawyer. As a child, young Walter contracted polio which left him lame for the rest of his life. The family moved to newly completed George Square in 1778 and Scott attended the burgh's High School. He trained as a lawyer and in time became the Clerk to the Court of Session. As a 15 year old he had a brief meeting with Robert Burns at Sciennes House when the poet paid his first visit to Edinburgh in the winter of 1786-1787.

Sir Walter Scott

Scott came from a well-known family from the Scottish Borders. He developed a passion for tales and legends from his native land. His first published works were however poems rather than stories. In 1802 he wrote *'Minstrelsy of the Scottish Border'* followed by *'The Lay of the Last Minstrel'*, then *'Marmion'* and in 1810, his best known poem *'Lady of the Lake'*. He now turned his hand to the writing of historical novels. *'Waverley'*, a tale of the 1745 - 1746 Jacobite Rebellion, was published in 1814 with tremendous success. Other titles followed in quick succession some credited to *'the author of Waverley'*. However the real identity of the author was kept secret. Jane Austen though was not fooled. In a letter of 1814 it seems that she was not best pleased with Scott!

"Walter Scott has no business to write novels, especially good ones. It is not fair. He has Fame and Profit enough as a Poet and should not be taking the bread out of other people's mouths. I do not like him and don't mean to like 'Waverley' if I can help it but fear I must."

While many suspected that Scott wrote the stories, it was not until 1827, as mentioned previously, that Scott finally acknowledged that he was indeed the author of what had become known as *'The Waverley Novels.'* In all, twenty-six titles were written. Scott enjoyed tremendous success with such tales as *'Rob Roy'*, *Kenilworth* and *'Ivanhoe'*. One of Scott's most successful books was *'The Heart of Midlothian'*, a story based on the infamous Porteous Riot that took place in Edinburgh in 1736, when the Captain of the Town Guard, John Porteous, was lynched by a mob in the Grassmarket.

At one time he was earning in excess of £10,000 a year from his writing. In 1811 he purchased the little farmhouse of Abbotsford near Melrose beside the River Tweed in his beloved Scottish Borders and set about converting it into a grand stately home that can still be visited today.

Abbotsford

Scott was responsible for obtaining Royal permission for Edinburgh Castle to be searched for the long-lost Honours of Scotland.. There was a tremendous outpouring of rejoicing when the ancient Crown, Sceptre and Sword of State were discovered in a locked box on 4th February 1818, in the old Crown Room of the Castle. Scott later described the scene:

"The joy was therefore extreme when, the ponderous lid having been forced open....the regalia were discovered lying at the bottom covered with linen cloths as they had been left in 1707."

Scott was knighted for his services. He masterminded the Royal Visit of King George IV in 1822. Disaster though struck in 1826 when his publishing house, Ballantyne's, collapsed with losses of £120,000. Scott felt honour-bound to repay his share of the debts. He was forced to give up his beloved Abbotsford into the care of trustees and to sell this house in Castle Street.

*The Discovery of the lost Honours of Scotland 1817
(Walter Scott stands on the right holding the cloth)*

On that sad day, 15th March, 1826 Scott wrote in his diary:

*"This morning I leave number 39 Castle Street for the last time.
What a portion of my life has been spent there! It has sheltered me
from the prime of life to its decline and I must now bid goodbye to
it. So farewell poor number 39!"*

Scott moved into lodgings in St. David Street where he
continued to write to try to clear his debts. As a break from
writing his historical novels, Scott started work on his *'Tales
of a Grandfather'* in 1827 for his beloved six year old
grandson, John Hugh Lockhart, nicknamed Hugh Littlejohn
by his grandfather. Sadly the little boy died in 1831 and the
series of stories was left unfinished. By now Scott was in
poor health, worn out by overwork. A cruise to Europe was
cut short and he was brought back to die in his beloved
Abbotsford in 1832. Scott is buried in Dryburgh Abbey.

Looking along George Street to Charlotte Square c1829

MAP 4

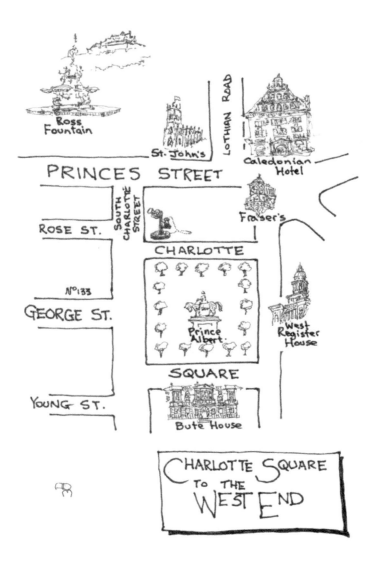

Now make your way westwards along George Street towards Charlotte Square. Look out on the north side for No. 133. In the early 1800s this was the home of Sir John Sinclair of Ulbster in Caithness.

Sir John was born in Thurso Castle, Caithness in 1756. He studied Law at Glasgow, Edinburgh and Oxford Universities and was admitted to both the Scottish and English Bars. He had a passionate interest in improving agriculture in Scotland. He was the first to introduce Cheviot sheep and in 1793, founded the Scottish Board of Agriculture to promote agricultural improvement. In 1784 he published his *'History of the Revenue of the British Empire'*. His many talents were recognised and he was a Fellow of both the Royal Society of London and of Edinburgh.

Amongst his achievements was the creation of *'The First Statistical Account of Scotland'* which was published by William Creech whom we met at the start of your tour, in which the word *'statistics'* was used for the first time. This was a most ambitious enterprise.

Sinclair, at his own expense, wrote to every Church of Scotland parish minister (there were more than 900 of them!) and asked them to reply to a series of questions about their parish. In all he listed 160 questions that he asked the ministers to answer. He was interested to know about such things as location, population, agriculture, industry, education, climate, significant changes since 1760, any events of note and so on. The returns from the parish ministers were published as they arrived back to Sir John. In all twenty-one volumes were produced between 1791 and 1799. These give a unique insight into life in Scotland at the end of the 18th century.

The Scottish Patriot.

Sir John Sinclair

Sir John served for many years as an MP and was a member of the Privy Council. He was a financial adviser to Prime Minister William Pitt during the French Revolutionary War. He died in 1835.

Sir John had a very large family and had to move from Charlotte Square to this bigger house round the corner in George Street. He had two children by his first wife and thirteen by his second! Like their father, the children were all very tall, either just below or over six feet! It must have been quite a sight to see them on their way out together. Their neighbours joked that the pavement in front of their house in George Street should be renamed *'The Giants' Causeway.'*

The North Side of Charlotte Square

Charlotte Square is the finest square in Edinburgh and has been designated as part of a World Heritage Site by UNESCO. Work started on Charlotte Square in 1792 with Robert Adam appointed as architect. He died though later that year but much of his original plan was implemented.

The northern side was designed to look like the front of a palace with a grand entrance in the middle (No. 6). In fact there are eleven separate houses here. Again you can see clear evidence of the popular classical style with the Corinthian columns and the sphinxes on the roof.

By now, the Town Council had relaxed its regulations to allow for larger windows and entrances. Whereas the first New Town houses had been rather plain in appearance, these houses had imposing entrance lobbies decorated with individual fan windows. There is also variety in the appearance of the finished stonework with the ground floor and above being of dressed ashlar while the servants' quarters below ground level were of rusticated stone.

The Entrance to Bute House, No 6 Charlotte Square

The first house to be completed (No. 6) was bought by Mr Orlando Hart, originally a shoemaker and now a member of the Town Council and Deacon of the Guild of Cordiners. The house cost £10,000, a colossal sum in those days. (About £1,000,000 today). Bloom though never got to enjoy his new property as he died in 1792 before the house was completed.

A study of the earliest residents of Charlotte Square confirms that the New Town had indeed attracted some of the wealthiest families not just of Edinburgh but indeed the whole of Scotland. John Lamond of Lamond (a Highland Clan Chief) lived in No. 7. The National Trust for Scotland has restored his house to how it would have looked in the 1790s and is well worth a visit. Sir John Sinclair moved into No. 6; in No. 13 lived Sir William Fettes, the wealthy Edinburgh tea merchant who made his fortune during the Napoleonic Wars and who founded Fettes College the well-known Edinburgh public school and in No. 24 the future Field Marshall Sir Douglas Haig was born in 1861.

Henry, Lord Cockburn

Henry, Lord Cockburn, a leading judge moved into No. 16 in 1812. His memoirs *'Memorials of his Time'*, published in 1856 shortly after his death, give a colourful account of Edinburgh life in the early 19th century. Cockburn served as Solicitor General for Scotland and promoted the Reform Bill of 1832 which extended the franchise. He was appointed as a judge in 1834. Cockburn was an early conservationist and his name is preserved in *'The Cockburn Association'*, a leading Edinburgh conservationist organisation. Cockburn Street, which runs northwards from the High Street, is named in his honour. He died in 1854 and is buried in Dean Cemetery.

In his *'Memorials'*, Cockburn gives his own recollections of living through that famous *'Golden Age'* for the City. He was very conscious that the appearance of Edinburgh had changed dramatically during his long lifetime. In one of his best passages, Cockburn recalls those early days living in Charlotte Square, just before work began developing the open farmlands lying to the north.

"It was then an open field of as green turf as Scotland could boast of, with a few respectable trees on the flat and thickly wooded along the water of Leith...That well-kept and almost evergreen field was the most beautiful piece of ground in immediate connection with the town and led the eye agreeably over to our distant northern scenery... But how can I forget the glory of that scene on the still nights...I have stood in Queen Street or the opening of the north-west corner of Charlotte Square, and listened to the ceaseless rural corn-craiks nestling happily in the dewy grass."

A decorative Sphinx in Charlotte Square

The famous Scottish surgeon, James Syme lived in No. 9 and was followed there by his son-in-law Joseph Lister the pioneer of antiseptic surgery. Nos. 5, 6 and 7 were gifted to the National Trust for Scotland by The Earl of Bute in lieu of death duties in 1947. No. 6, known as Bute House, is the official residence of the First Minister of Scotland, the leader of the Scottish Government at Holyrood. No. 7 has been faithfully restored and furnished by the National Trust as it would have been in the 1790s when it was the home of the Lamond family. Known as *'The Georgian House'*, No. 7 tells the fascinating story of what life was like for those early residents of the first New Town. It is open to the public and well worth a visit.

Cross over to No. 7 and see if you can spot in the street outside, the iron manhole that covers the coal hole; the foot-scrapers to take the mud of your shoes and the sconces, on the railings beside the steps, used to extinguish the torches of the servants who had escorted you to the house.

West Register House (formally St. George's Church)

What was St George's Church stands at the west end of the Square. Robert Reid's design replaced that of Robert Adam. Work commenced in 1811 and was completed in 1814. Those familiar with St Paul's Cathedral in London will see a similarity in the dome but on a much smaller scale. In 1964, the church was closed and the building is now West Register House. Robert Reid was responsible for the design of many of the streets of Edinburgh's northern New Town. Interestingly he was permitted to design his own house, No. 44, in Charlotte Square.

Finally Charlotte Square Gardens are the setting for the annual Edinburgh International Book Festival. It is claimed to be the largest festival of its kind in the world. The statue in the Gardens is of Prince Albert, husband of Queen Victoria. He died, probably of typhoid fever, in December 1861. One of his last public duties had been to lay the foundation stone for what is now the National Museum of Scotland in Chambers Street. The statue, sculpted by Sir John Steell, was unveiled by Queen Victoria in August 1867. The widowed Queen knighted Steell for his work.

Charlotte Square Gardens during the Book Festival

Now head south out of Charlotte Square towards Princes Street by way of South Charlotte Street. Alexander Graham Bell, the inventor of the telephone, was born here at No. 16 in 1847. Bell developed a passionate interest in sound. He emigrated to Canada in 1870 and from there moved to Boston. He continued with his experimental work and in 1876 patented the telephone and in 1877 formed the Bell Telephone Company. Bell also did pioneering work in developing the phonograph and powered flight. He invented the world's first metal detector in 1881. Bell was showered with honours, dying in Nova Scotia in 1922.

Cross over Princes Street and on your left facing you, is the statue of Sir James Young Simpson, the discoverer of the anaesthetic properties of chloroform, whose house we saw at No. 52 Queen Street.

While it has been estimated that no less than £3 million had been spent on the first phase of Edinburgh's New Town, there was a consequence that had perhaps not been fully anticipated by the City Fathers. Where at first, wealthy Edinburgh folk had been reluctant to leave the cosy familiarity of the Old Town, now there was a rush to buy the beautiful, spacious new houses. Within a generation, those who could afford it had abandoned the Old Town. Where before better-off and the more humble folk had shared a common stair in the tenements of the Royal Mile, now increasingly these were the homes of the poor.

Writing in 1833, Robert Chambers noted that with the building of the New Town, Edinburgh had changed socially:

"Edinburgh is in fact two towns in more ways than one. It contains an upper and under town – the one a sort of thoroughfare for the children of business and fashion, the other a den of retreat for the poor, the diseased and the ignorant."

Below you are West Princes Street Gardens, extending for 29 acres. These attractive public gardens were laid out after the Nor' Loch was drained. Originally owned by the Princes Street householders, the Gardens were bought for the City in 1876. The Gardens, with the wonderful backdrop of the Castle Rock, are the setting for the spectacular annual Fireworks' Concert which traditionally marks the end of the Edinburgh International Festival.

West Princes Street Gardens and the Ross Fountain

A beautiful feature in the Gardens is the Ross Fountain. This was designed by a Frenchman M. Durenne and was built for the Paris International Exhibition of 1862. It was bought by Daniel Ross, an Edinburgh gunsmith who shipped the fountain back to Edinburgh in 122 pieces; reassembled it and gifted the fountain to the City. Further east you can see the Ross Bandstand gifted to Edinburgh in 1877 by William Ross, the Chairman of the Distillers Company, the leading Scotch Whisky producer of the day.

Now head back towards what generations of Edinburgh folk have called *'The West End'*. Indeed the earliest reference to the *'West End'* was probably made by the English traveller Edward Topham who visited Edinburgh in 1774. He wrote:

"(The New Town) is terminated at each end by two very elegant and extensive squares; that on the East End is called St Andrew Square, the other, not yet finished, Charlotte Square. Princes Street is the most southerly, and extends from the Northern extremity of the Bridge (the North Bridge) quite to the West End of the Town."

The church on the corner is St John's Episcopal Church built in 1818 to a design of William Burn. The building was funded by the Edinburgh banker Sir William Forbes. To the south lies St Cuthbert's Church. A church has stood here for some 1200 years. St Cuthbert was a 7th century churchman associated with the abbeys of Melrose and Lindisfarne. The church was extensively rebuilt at the end of the 19th century, the work of the Edinburgh architect Hippolytus Blanc.

St John's Episcopal Church

On the other side of Princes Street is one of Edinburgh's best-known department stores. The present building dating from 1935 was for many years, Maules the Clothier. *"Meet me at Maules"* was a popular Edinburgh rendezvous. In 1934 the premises were taken over by Binns and then in 1976 by House of Fraser. In 2022 this will reopen as the Johnnie Walker Whisky Experience.

The House of Fraser Store at the West End

Across the road is the famous 'Caley Hotel'. Just as Craig's original New Town was balanced by two squares, so Princes Street was 'balanced' by what originally were two railway stations and two railway hotels, the North British (now the Balmoral) at the East End served the Waverley Station for the North British Railway Company and here, the Caledonian or Caley Hotel. The hotel was opened in 1903. It was built for the Caledonian Railway Company to provide first-class hotel accommodation for passengers arriving at the neighbouring Caledonian Station. The first station had been built here as early as 1848. The station was closed in 1965 and demolished four years later.

Both Edinburgh residents and visitors alike were conscious that there was something very special about the New Town. An English visitor, Robert Heron, writing at the end of the 1790s, recorded that:

"With regard to the buildings that have of late arisen in this City with such incredible rapidity, we may venture to say, that, in regularity and magnificence, they are scarcely equalled, or at least not excelled, by any in Europe...When Charlotte Square, at the west end of George Street, shall be completed, this City will certainly surpass, in regularity and magnificence, every other in Great Britain."

Here we end your New Town Tour. The street that you are standing on, Princes Street, is one of the best-known streets in the world. For some 250 years Edinburgh folk and visitors alike have gone about their business under the watchful eye of the majestic Edinburgh Castle.

Princes Street c 1912

INDEX

FURTHER READING

Arnot, Hugo: *The History of Edinburgh*

Birrell, J. F.: *An Edinburgh Alphabet*

Catford, F. E.: *Edinburgh. The Story of a City*

Chambers, Robert: *Traditions of Edinburgh*

Cockburn, Henry: *Memorials of his Time*

Coghill, Hamish: *Lost Edinburgh*

Cosh, Mary: *Edinburgh the Golden Age*

Grant, James: *Old and New Edinburgh*

Harris, Stuart; *The Place Names of Edinburgh* Massie, Alan: *Edinburgh*

Melvin, Eric: *The Edinburgh of John Kay*

Melvin, Eric: *A Walk Down Edinburgh's Royal Mile*

Ritchie, W. K.: *Edinburgh in the Golden Age*

Wilson, Sir Daniel: *Memorials of Edinburgh in the Olden Time*

Youngson, A. J.: *The Making of Classical Edinburgh*

Some of these titles are out of print. A good source for locating such titles is: www.abebooks.co.uk

ABOUT THE AUTHOR

Eric Melvin graduated with First Class Honours in History and Political Thought from Edinburgh University in 1967. He qualified as a Secondary teacher of History and Modern Studies. He retired from teaching in 2005, working latterly as Headteacher at Currie Community High School.

In addition to teaching History at school, Eric has for many years taken Community Education classes for The City of Edinburgh in both Scottish History and The History of Edinburgh. He also give talks to various groups on aspects of the City's History. (e.g. Probus and Local History Clubs). Eric is a trained volunteer guide for The Edinburgh Festival Voluntary Guides Association and regularly takes groups down the Royal Mile and through the New Town

Eric has had several books published for younger readers on aspects of Scottish History. He is the author of the companion volume 'A Walk Down Edinburgh's Royal Mile.'

Eric is a member of the High Constables of Edinburgh, the historic bodyguard of Edinburgh's Lord Provost who act as an escort on ceremonial occasions. He works voluntarily in the Oxfam Bookshop at Morningside and has done voluntary teaching in Chogoria Girls' High School in Kenya.

Eric is married to Lynda, a retired Nursery School Teacher. They have two sons, John currently lecturing in Heritage Tourism at Hosei University in Tokyo and Graeme, also working in Tokyo as a Business Communications Skills Trainer for American Express. John is married to Shizue Ichikawa from Sakata in Japan. They are the proud parents of Isla, a first grand-child, born in August 2010 and Rui born in April 2013.